HOT 'N' THROBBING

BY
PAULA VOGEL

★

★

DRAMATISTS
PLAY SERVICE
INC.

HOT 'N' THROBBING
Copyright © 1993, 1995, 2000, Paula Vogel

All Rights Reserved

SPECIAL NOTE

HOT 'N' THROBBING was first workshopped at Circle Repertory Theatre,
New York, in October 1992.

Originally produced by the American Repertory Theatre, Cambridge, Massachusetts:
Robert Brustein, Artistic Director; Robert J. Orchard, Managing Director.

Subsequently produced by Arena Stage, Washington, D.C.
Molly Smith, Artistic Director; Stephen Richard, Executive Director.

HOT 'N' THROBBING was made possible by generous grants and residencies from the
National Endowment for the Arts Playwriting Fellowship, a fellowship from the
Bunting Institute, Radcliffe College, and residencies at the
Rockefeller Foundation at Bellagio Center, Italy, and the Yaddo Colony.

HOT 'N' THROBBING was awarded a major grant from the Fund for New American
Plays, a project of the John F. Kennedy Center for the Performing Arts with support
from American Express Company, in cooperation with the President's Committee on
the Arts and the Humanities. Major support was also provided by the
Educational Foundation of America.

The current version of HOT 'N' THROBBING was produced by Arena Stage (Molly Smith, Artistic Director) in Washington, D.C., on September 3, 1999. It was directed by Molly Smith; the set design was by Bill C. Ray; the lighting design was by Allen Lee Hughes; the sound design was by Timothy M. Thompson; the costume design was by Marilyn Salvatore; and the stage manager was Barbara Rollins. The cast was as follows:

VOICE-OVER	Sue Jin Song
CHARLENE	Lynnda Ferguson
LESLIE ANN	Rhea Seehorn
THE VOICE	Craig Wallace
CALVIN	Danny Pintauro
CLYDE	Colin Lane

HOT 'N' THROBBING was originally produced by American Repertory Theatre (Robert Brustein, Artistic Director; Robert J. Orchard, Managing Director) in Cambridge, Massachusetts, on April 14, 1994. It was directed by Anne Bogart; the set design was by Christine Jones; the lighting design was by John Ambrosone; the sound design and original music were by Christopher Walker; the costume design was by Jenny Fulton; and the stage manager was Ruth E. Sternberg. The cast was as follows:

VOICE-OVER	Alexandra Loria
WOMAN	Diane D'Aquila
GIRL	Amy Louise Lammert
VOICE	Royal Miller
BOY	Randall Jaynes
MAN	Jack Willis

Some plays only daughters can write.

Hot 'N' Throbbing was written on a National Endowment for the Arts fellowship — because obscenity begins at home.

CHARACTERS

LESLIE ANN (aka Layla), about fifteen.

CALVIN, about fourteen.

Both Calvin and Leslie Ann are voyeurs, as teenagers are, hooked on watching — TV, Nintendo, music videos, parents. They watch the live action.

CHARLENE, about forty. Wears Lina Wertmuller glasses. On-again, off-again member of Weight Watchers and Al Anon.

CLYDE, over forty. Holes in dungarees. Almost a beer belly. (Note to actor: You've got to go gang-busters on this role. The bigger the asshole you are, the more we'll love you. Trust me on this.)

VOICE-OVER: Hard to tell her age under the red lights. Voice-Over narrates the script that the Woman is writing. She's Charlene's inner voice. She is a sex-worker; at times bored with her job; at times, emphatically over-acting, hoping to land a job in a legitimate film. Sometimes she dances. Her voice is amplified through a microphone. Her voice is sensual and husky.

THE VOICE: The first level — he's a character in Charlene's screenplay, a detective. At times he's a client in the strip joint, watching the Voice-Over with appreciation or jaded disinterest. His voice is also amplified through a microphone. He waits for the coroner to arrive and the forensics squad. While he waits, he reads Charlene's books — German, French, Irish dialects, or not — maybe just a flat Baltimore dialect. Sometimes he's the D.J. — spinning the score of the play. He becomes Clyde's alter-ego. And he's also the director of a Gyno film gone bad.

SET

There are two play worlds in this piece. The stage lights and the red lights — reality, constructed as we know it, and a world that sometimes resembles the real — as we fantasize about it.

In the red light, the living room becomes the film set of Gyno productions, a strip joint, a dance hall. The red light arenas and the living room have this in common: They are stages for performance, for viewing.

Don't believe anything that happens in the red light.

The living room should look like the living room of a townhouse that cost $79,900 ten years ago. On a 9 1/2% mortgage, no deposit down. Although we never see the upstairs, we know there are two bedrooms, one bath; downstairs there is a half-bath. These pre-constructed developments are called "empty-nesters."

A few pieces. A sofa which folds out, in a tweed. Scotch-guarded. A matching arm chair. A coffee table. Television sets, which may or may not be running erotica or police shows. All the sets are on constantly.

The door to the half-bath. A front door. On the lower stage left, a large white office desk complex, with a secretary, holding a computer and printer. Along the wall behind this office-island, where the dining room was supposed to be, are the ubiquitous sliding patio doors, looking out onto the parking lot in a Maryland suburb. Curtains pre-made, cream that sort of matches the tweed. And oh yes, wall-to-wall shag.

On the other side of the sliding patio doors, a red ramp that curves its way out into the audience — a runway/dance area or a podium.

TIME

Ten years ago and ten years from now.

MUSIC

I wrote this play in 1993 to several sound-tracks: Janet Jackson's "Control" (particularly "Nasty") and Kaoma's "World Beat." Also "Thriller" and "Silence of the Lambs" sound-tapes from horror movies and Frank Sinatra. The main thing is that the music changes from erotic to terrorific.

In 1999 I write this to "Red Hot + Blue."

PROPS

Red light where indicated.
And music. Music always helps to get it up.

HOT 'N' THROBBING

(In a growing **red light**, we see Leslie Ann dressed in very tight pants and a halter top, making suggestive stripper or vogue-ing movements. At end of **Voice-Over**, we see an older woman sitting at a computer screen, typing. Living room.)

V.O.
CUT TO: INTERIOR. NIGHT. VOICE-OVER:
"She was hot. She was throbbing. But she was in control. Control of her body. Control of her thoughts. Control of ... him."

"He was hot. He was throbbing. And out of control. He needed to be restrained. Tied Down. And taught a Lesson.

"But not hurt. Not too much. Just ... enough. She would make his flesh red all over. She would raise the blood with her loving discipline. And she would make him wait. Make him beg. Make them both wait ... until she was ready."

CHARLENE AND VOICE-OVER:
And she would make him wait. Make him beg.
CHARLENE:
(Types)
Sounds too male-bashing. — "Make him ask?" Oh, fuck it. "Make him beg ... make them both beg ... "
(Suddenly the bathroom door slams open in **stage light.** Leslie Ann stands in front of the sink dressed as above.)
LESLIE ANN:
(Screams)
MAAHM! WHERE'S YOUR EYELINER?

CHARLENE:
ON THE TOP SHELF! NEXT TO THE BEN GAY!
(Back to the flat narrative tone at the computer)
"Until she was ready. Ready release them both at the end of a long, hard night. Ready to heave herself to the other side of her love throes, ready to give it up — "
LESLIE ANN:
MAAHM! CAN I USE YOUR MASCARA!!
CHARLENE:
Sounds like upchucking. "Ready to pant, ready to scream, ready to die in each other's arms ... "
(Charlene stops; calls out:)
Leslie Ann! What are you doing?
LESLIE ANN:
Puttin' on some make-up.
CHARLENE:
Why are you putting on make-up.
LESLIE ANN:
I already told you.
CHARLENE:
No you did not tell me.
LESLIE ANN:
I Did. So.
CHARLENE:
Why are you wearing make-up.
LESLIE ANN:
I'm Going. Out.
CHARLENE:
Out Where?
LESLIE ANN:
Out. To Lisa's. To Spend the Night.
CHARLENE:
This is the first time I've heard about it.
LESLIE ANN:
I Told You!
CHARLENE:
I don't want you going to Lisa's.

LESLIE ANN:
But why?!
CHARLENE:
Because. I. said. so.
LESLIE ANN:
I'm goin'.
CHARLENE:
Her parents do not supervise that young lady. You are not going to Lisa's.
LESLIE ANN:
But all the girls will be there!
CHARLENE:
You are not all the girls.
(Leslie Ann slams the bathroom door. We hear the water running. From offstage:)
LESLIE ANN
(Off)
I'M GOING!
(Charlene sighs. Types)
(**Red Light.** The Voice and Voice-Over simulate/dance with the monologue below; Calvin enters, sits on the sofa, watching the TV. Leslie Ann emerges from the bathroom in her tight pants. She slumps next to her brother, watching the TV, blase and waiting.)

V.O.
VOICE-OVER CONTINUED:
He wanted to take her downtown and book her.
Spread her, cuff her and search every inch.
He wanted to penetrate her secrets
with his will. He wanted to gently pry open that
sweet channel that leads to joy, and fill her with
his passion until the dull pain faded into pleasure.
Until her hips locked into a rhythm to match his.
Together they would rock each other, clinging to
each other as the tempo got faster, faster, faster
and faster, faster and faster and faster, faster ...

(The Voice and V.O. break and retreat to the background; **lights** go

11

back to normal. Calvin slumps on the sofa, Leslie Ann confronts Charlene:)

LESLIE ANN:

You just don't care. You want me to stay in this boring house until I rot like you and four-eyes on the sofa over there.

CHARLENE:

Leslie Ann, I am behind my schedule. I've got to get out forty pages by the first mail tomorrow morning, and I'm on page twenty-six.

LESLIE ANN:

Layla. I am not answering to a dumb-shit name like Leslie Ann.

CALVIN:

(singing the Eric Clapton riff &:)

"LAY-LA!! YOU'VE GOT ME ON MY KNEES." [1]

LESLIE ANN:

(appealing to her mother for help against Calvin)

MAH-HM.

CHARLENE:

(still typing)

I'm sorry, sweetie. Layla.

CALVIN:

"LAY-LA! I'M BEGGING DARLIN', PLEASE."

LESLIE ANN:

Shut up, creep!

CALVIN:

Are you going out in those tight pants?

LESLIE ANN:

What business is it of yours?

CALVIN

Those pants are so tight you can see your P.L.s.

LESLIE ANN:

Shut up.

(Charlene looks up from typing with interest)

CHARLENE:

What are P.L.s?

(No Answer)

LESLIE ANN:

Nothin'.

(Charlene back to typing)

CALVIN:
Hey, as long as I don't have to walk you up the aisle for some shotgun wedding, you trouncing around with your P.L.s hanging out ...

CHARLENE:
P.L.s?

LESLIE ANN:
Why don't you just go beat-off in your room, you little pervo ...

CHARLENE:
Those pants are too tight. Did you spray-paint them on?

LESLIE ANN:
Betcha wish you had my thighs, huh, ma?

CHARLENE:
We are not discussing the subject of my thighs. You are not leaving the house dressed like that.

LESLIE ANN:
Huh. That's funny. Coming from you.

CHARLENE:
What's that supposed to mean?

LESLIE ANN:
Nothin'.

CHARLENE:
I could kill your father for telling you kids a thing like that. I do not write *pornography*. There's a mile of difference between that and ... *adult entertainment*. He wouldn't know the difference.

CALVIN
I think it's cool.

LESLIE ANN:
Shut up, Toady. (To Charlene:) So what's the difference?

CHARLENE:
What?

LESLIE ANN:
What's the big difference between porno and —

CHARLENE:
It's only pornography when women and gays and minorities try to take control of their own imaginations. No one blinks an eye when men do it.

LESLIE ANN:

Uh-huh. So it's okay that you objectify my body because you happen to be female?

CHARLENE:

Who have you been talking to?

CALVIN:

It was in her Problems of Democracy class this week.

LESLIE ANN:

Your movies are filled with girls my age as sex objects — why don't you use women your own age?

CALVIN:

(to his sister)

'Cause no one would pay to see that.

CHARLENE:

You're going out of the house dressed like that and you blame me for making you a sex object?!

LESLIE ANN:

That's right, that's right, blame the victim!

(Charlene counts to ten)

CHARLENE:

I know what you're doing. Using this as a ploy for me to lose my temper. And it's not working, Leslie Ann. You are not going to Lisa's. You are staying home and reading a book.

(Leslie Ann stalks to her mother's bookshelves; the Voice suddenly gets interested. He'll start to peruse the books)

LESLIE ANN:

Books like the porno you read?

CHARLENE:

I'd rather have you read Henry Miller or D.H. Lawrence than watch *Texas Chainsaw Massacre*.

LESLIE ANN:

Texas Chainsaw Massacre is a lot less boring.

V.O.

Come on, Charlene. Twenty-six pages.

CHARLENE:

This is not about me. You will not fling … the way I. make. a.

living into my face every time I. give. you. a. directive. The way
I put food on the plate, and Reeboks on the feet. You are not
leaving this house, period, young lady. I want you to go upstairs
to your room and do some homework for a change. Your grades
last quarter were a disgrace.

LESLIE ANN:
Calvin gets to go out.

CHARLENE:
Calvin has a 3.75. Calvin can go out all he wants on a Friday
night. You are staying home and opening up a book. You'll like it.
Moby Dick. I loved that book.

CALVIN:
Her book report's due Monday.

V.O.
(calling)
Charlene.

CHARLENE:
You children can read quietly in your rooms. I've got to get this
section done. Go on upstairs and open up your books.

CALVIN:
The only thing Leslie Ann wants to open is her P.L.s

CHARLENE:
Calvin! Quit picking on your sister!

LESLIE ANN:
Get your little tattletale nose out of my P.L.s, you creep!

CHARLENE:
I'VE HAD IT! What are you talking about? Leslie Ann?

LESLIE ANN:
Ask Calvin. Go ahead, little brother, tell mom what you've been
calling me.

CHARLENE:
Calvin?
(No response)
I asked you a question.

CALVIN:
P.L.s are a name for a girl's ... you know.

15

LESLIE ANN:

It's not very nice. You know, for an honor roll creep, you sure use some nice language.

CHARLENE:

When I was growing up, I didn't have a room of my own. And so I was determined that my children would each have their own privacy. Your Mother sleeps on a convertible sofa that has to be made up each morning so you can have your own space. I want you both to go upstairs to your rooms, if you can't be quiet and act normal down here.

LESLIE ANN:

Some privacy. The walls are paper-thin. How can I concentrate when all I can hear is four-eyes beating off?

CALVIN:

I do not! You have the mouth of a slut, Leslie Ann!

LESLIE ANN:

You beat off! In the catcher's mitt Daddy gave you for Christmas! I can feel the walls shaking! —

(The Voice-Over tosses a leather catcher's mitt to the Voice)

CHARLENE:

(suddenly interested, making notes):

Catcher's mitt. Open Window. Show Clipboard. Notes: Leather Catcher's mitt —

CALVIN:

Mind Your Own Business!

LESLIE ANN:

That's not what Dad meant when he said practice. Catching pop-up flies —

CALVIN:

Shut up! —

LESLIE ANN:

That's why you wear glasses, Calvin. Nobody else in this family does, little brother. 'Cause you violate yourself.

CALVIN:

Mom wears glasses!

(Startled, the two teenagers suddenly look at their mother with a horrifying new idea. Charlene, oblivious, stares into her computer screen, typing with a vengeance. The Voice fists the catcher's mitt.

16

The siblings stop and erupt in laughter.)
LESLIE ANN:
Shut up, pervo!
CALVIN:
Musta learned it from you, P.L. —
LESLIE ANN:
Quit calling me that, and I might just learn you something interesting —
CALVIN:
Yeah?
(They both look at their mother, deep into her typing)
LESLIE ANN:
Yeah. So you won't haveta hang in the bushes outside the house. You do, don'tcha?
(Calvin is suddenly quiet, beet red.)
Yeah. I thought that was you.
(Leslie Ann suddenly wrestles her brother into a lock on the sofa, on top of him, his arm twisted)
CALVIN (hissed):
Shit!
LESLIE ANN: (whispered):
Watching me undressing. in the bushes. Straight-A student. I'm going to teach. you. a. lesson —
(Charlene types on)
CALVIN
You're.An.Asshole!
LESLIE ANN:
What.Did.You.Call.Me?
CALVIN:
Stop it!
LESLIE ANN:
I'll stop when I. feel. like. it.
(The Voice finds a passage in one of the books and reads it to the Voice-Over as Leslie Ann torments her brother)
THE VOICE:
"Lolita, light of my life, fire of my loins. My sin, my soul. Lo-lee-ta." [2]
(There is the sound of an automobile horn. Loud)
"Lo. Lee. Ta."

(The horn imitates The Voice. Three times. Leslie Ann jumps up from the sofa.)
LESLIE ANN:
That's my ride! Mom! I've got to go.
CHARLENE:
You are not leaving this house. Young Lady.
LESLIE ANN:
You said I could!
CHARLENE:
When! When did I say that?
(Voice-Over lights a cigarette, bored. She puffs. The Voice reads)
LESLIE ANN:
Last night. I asked you. And you said you didn't care what I did. So I told Lisa yes.
CHARLENE:
Is that Lisa outside? I don't like you riding with her. Go out and tell her I. said. no.
LESLIE ANN:
You said you need peace and quiet. I'm going to give you some. It's an overnight. A slumber party. I'll be back tomorrow.

V.O.
Bye Bye.

CHARLENE.
You march upstairs. Right. this. minute. You are not leaving this house — (Once more, the car horn trumpets: Lo-lee-ta.)
LESLIE ANN:
I'll see you!
(Leslie Ann rushes to the door, exits and slams it behind her. There is a pause. Calvin watches Charlene. She returns to her computer.)
CHARLENE:
Oh, Jesus. I could use a cigarette.
CALVIN:
You quit smoking.
CHARLENE:
I know. I miss it at times like this. Jesus Christ. Page ... twenty-seven.

CALVIN:
Thirteen to go.
CHARLENE:
What's on your agenda for tonight?
CALVIN:
I'm staying here with you, mom.
CHARLENE:
Nothing's going to happen.
CALVIN:
I know.
CHARLENE:
Because if you want to go out, you should just go ahead —
CALVIN:
I don't want to. I'm just going to sit here, quietly, and read *Moby Dick* again, all right?
CHARLENE:
I don't want you to write Leslie Ann's book report for her, all right?
CALVIN:
All right.
(Charlene stares at the computer screen. Calvin stares at her. Charlene looks up and sees him staring.)

V.O.
"What are you looking at?"
THE VOICE:
What are you —

V.O.
"looking — "

THE VOICE:
— looking at?
(Calvin looks down at his book, quickly. Charlene goes back to the screen. Calvin stares at her again. Charlene tentatively starts to type. Stops. Starts again. Stops.)

V.O.
"What are you looking at?

THE VOICE:
What are you —

V.O.
                     "looking — "

THE VOICE:
— looking at?
CALVIN:
Writer's block, Mom?
CHARLENE:
I'm running out of words.
CALVIN:
How about …
THE VOICE:
(whispered)
— Throbbing —
CALVIN:
— Throbbing?
CHARLENE:
Don't make fun of me, son. My writing puts food in your mouth.
CALVIN:
I wasn't making fun! I was just trying to help!
CHARLENE:
I know. I'm sorry. Maybe after you go to college, you'll be able to be a real writer. Great writers can see into the future. I'd really like that.
CALVIN:
You're the writer in the family.
CHARLENE:
Oh Lord. Not this — this is just … junk.
CALVIN:
(in a rush)
No it's not — I really like —
(Calvin covers his mouth)
CHARLENE:
Calvin Lee Dwyer. Have you been reading the files on my personal computer? That's not for you to read!
(beat)

How did you get my password!

CALVIN:

I just wanted to read it.

CHARLENE:

There is no privacy in this house.

(She can't help herself)

Do you really think — it's any good?

CALVIN:

I really like the detective, Mama. He's cool.

CHARLENE:

I'm kinda proud of the detective.

CALVIN:

Mama, I think you can really write.

CHARLENE:

Oh honey — not really. Not yet. Someday, maybe, when you kids are all taken care of — someday. I'd like to think I have one good book in me ... You could be a writer too.

CALVIN:

I don't want to be anything. And I'm not going to college.

CHARLENE:

We'll see.

CALVIN:

To Prince Georges Community? With all the geeks?

CHARLENE:

That's where I went, remember. But I meant maybe somewhere away from home. it would be good for you to get away.

CALVIN:

Leslie Ann's the one who wants to go away.

CHARLENE:

I worry sometimes that she'll get as far as the back seat of a car.

CALVIN:

I don't think so. I think she's scared to death ... (Pause. The Voice breathes heavily twice)

CHARLENE:

Why?

CALVIN:

No reason.

(Pause)

21

CHARLENE:
Okay.
(The Voice stops breathing)
Page twenty-seven … I need some words that pack a punch.
CALVIN:
So how about throbbing?
CHARLENE:
I've got throbbing all over the page. There are just so many ways to say throbbing …

V.O.
— "Pulsating — "

THE VOICE:
— "Beating — "

V.O.
"Heaving — "

THE VOICE:
— Battering — "
CHARLENE:
Wait a moment! Cut — Cut — Cut!! That's it, Charlene — Cut To — (**Light** changes to **red.** The Voice stands with a catcher's mitt.)

V.O.
"CUT TO: FLASHBACK. EXTERIOR. In the bushes outside the house. Nighttime. We see a YOUNG BOY, not yet old enough to shave. He is peering up through the bushes at: CUT TO: BOY's POINT OF VIEW. we see an attractive older WOMAN, full-hipped, through her bedroom window, looking at herself in the mirror. THE WOMAN removes her glasses, and gazes at her image."

(Charlene removes her glasses at the computer. Calvin stares at her.)

CUT TO: THE YOUNG BOY. Standing now. He watches as She strokes her face. We see him raise his hand, which holds a baseball mitt. He strokes the leather with his free hand, softly feeling the texture.

(The Voice follows the instructions of the Voice-Over.)

"CLOSE UP. On the mitt. THE BOY fists it several times, then raises the glove to his face, breathing in the leather.

(Calvin stares at The Voice hypnotically. The Voice tosses the catcher's mitt to Calvin, who dons it and follows the Voice-Over)

CUT TO: THE WOMAN, who begins to feel her own body.

CUT TO: YOUNG BOY, who begins to run the glove across his chest.

CUT TO: THE WOMAN, who closes her eyes and runs her fingers over her rounded hips, and down into her waistline.

(Bored, the Voice heads back to the bookshelves and picks up a book.)

CUT TO: CLOSE UP on leather mitt, rubbing up and down THE BOY'S blue-jeaned thighs —

CUT TO: —

(The Voice begins to read from *Moby Dick*)

THE VOICE:
"Yes, Ishmael, the same fate may be thine. But somehow I grew merry again. Yes, there is death in this business of whaling — But what then? Me thinks that what they call my shadow here on earth is my true substance." [3] (**Lights** change back. Calvin sits on the sofa, fondling his catcher's mitt)

CHARLENE:
What the heck was that? Shoot. I've lost it. "Cut to — Cut to ... cut to ... Fudge. Fiddlesticks.

CALVIN:
Something wrong, Mom?

CHARLENE:
I don't know. I'm distracted, I guess. Other voices are coming in over the airwaves.

V.O.
(Smoking)
"Cigarette. Lo-lee-ta. Cigarette."

CHARLENE:
Concentrate, Charlene. "Cut to — "

V.O.
"Do the dishes. Dishes. Dishes."

CHARLENE:
Oh, God. Time for a break. First — save, close, exit, quit. Power Down. Ah. (Charlene crosses to Calvin and sits beside him) You're not worried, are you Calvin?
CALVIN:
Nope.
CHARLENE:
Because I can take care of myself.
CALVIN:
Uh-huh.
(Charlene brushes the hair back off his forehead)
CHARLENE:
I'm sorry you saw ... what you saw.
CALVIN:
Yeah. But it was a good thing I was there.
CHARLENE:
Yes. it was. A very good thing. But it's never going to happen again.
CALVIN:
I know.
(Charlene goes to hug him; he stiffens, moves away, embarrassed)
CHARLENE:
How did you get to be so big so fast?
CALVIN:
Leslie Ann's still bigger.
CHARLENE:
You're catching up.
(Beat.)
You know what I miss? I miss the times when you would come

inside the house, as a little boy, with a scraped knee or in some ...
pain ... and you'd come in, crying, and let me hold you. Boys
grow up into men so quickly and we never get to just hold you.
Now you always squirm away.

CALVIN:

God, Mom.

(Pause)

CHARLENE:

Calvin?

CALVIN:

Yeah?

CHARLENE:

Where does your sister go on weekends?

CALVIN:

Ya know. Out.

CHARLENE:

Out where? Where does she go with Lisa?

(Red Light strikes the area outside of the sliding doors. Leslie Ann
and the Voice-Over do a slow, expert teasing dance for an imaginary
male clientele. Calvin parallels their movements.)

CALVIN:

Well ... see, first they hitch to Mount Pleasant with some subur-
ban father type in his Volvo station wagon. Then they hop on the
No. 42 bus to the Corner of Florida and Connecticut. They get off
by the bus stop, and walk two blocks east. They check to make
sure they're not being followed. Then they duck into this joint, it's
all red brick on the front, with the windows blacked out, except
for the Budweiser sign. The door is solid metal. They nod to the
bouncer, who always pats Leslie Ann on the fanny. They trot
behind the curtains in back of the bar, quick, see, so the clientele
won't see them in their street clothes. And backstage, Al, who's the
owner, yells at 'em for being late.

And they slip into this toilet of a dressing room, where they
strip off their jeans and sweats in such a hurry, they're inside out,
thrown in the corner. And they help each other into the scanty
sequins and the two inch heels.

And they slink out together in the blue light as the warm-up act,
and wrap their legs around the poles. And Al keeps an eye out on

25

the guys, who haven't got a buzz on yet, so they're pretty docile, 'cause the girls are jailbait. And Leslie Ann and her best friend Lisa shake it up for only one set. And before you know it, the twenty minutes are up, just a few half-hearted grabs, and they're doing full splits to scoop up the dollar bills that will pay for the midnight double feature at the mall and the burgers afterwards at Big Bob's. (**Red Light** out on Leslie Ann and Voice-Over. Charlene, who has been mesmerized, breaks out of her reverie.)

CHARLENE:
Calvin!

CALVIN:
Jesus, Mom. You're not the only one who can make up stories. Take a joke, will ya? She probably hangs out at Lisa's being dumb. (Pause.)

CHARLENE:
Don't you have a nice girl you can take to the movies tonight?

CALVIN:
I don't know any nice girls.

CHARLENE:
Well, how about calling up some of your friends and doing something with them?

CALVIN:
All the boys in school are creeps.

CHARLENE:
But it's Friday night!

CALVIN:
So?

CHARLENE:
Calvin, sweetie, it's not right for you to spend every weekend in the house.

CALVIN:
Am I bothering you?

CHARLENE:
That's not the point. You're never going to meet someone slumped on the sofa.

CALVIN:
I'm not slumping.

CHARLENE:
You are. Sit up straight; you're wearing the springs down that way
— when I was your age —
CALVIN:
(Agonized)
*What.*Do.You. *Want* From me?
CHARLENE:
I just want you to have some *Fun.*
CALVIN:
I'm going.
CHARLENE:
Where?
CALVIN:
What does it matter? I'm going. Out. I can't even sit in the privacy
of my own home —
CHARLENE:
Now wait, sweetie, I don't want you to take it like that —
CALVIN:
Jesus. I'm gone.
(Calvin stalks to the door, opens it and slams out.)
CHARLENE:
(Guiltily)
Have a nice time! Don't stay out. Too late ...
(Charlene goes back to the computer, and turns it on.)
Boot up. Password. Drive A.
(Charlene waits. Pauses. Charlene stealthily unlocks her desk
drawer, takes out a pack of cigarettes. Waits. Carefully selects one.
Fishes out matches from the drawer.
CHARLENE AND VOICE OVER:
Our little secret, Charlene.
(Charlene lights up. Starts to type.)

V.O.
"CUT TO: CLOSE UP:
She tentatively licked the tip, a gentle flick of the
tongue, before perching it on her lips. Her head
instinctively reared back, before its acid taste.
She gently sucked, letting it linger in her mouth —

she gently sucked — "

(Charlene pauses, reads that she wrote, inhales and exhales. The Voice reads *Moby Dick* aloud:)

THE VOICE:
"The Red Tide — "

V.O.
"She ... sucked ... the tip ... she ... "

THE VOICE:
"The red tide now poured from all sides of the monster like brooks down a hill."

CHARLENE:
Where is that coming from?

(Charlene begins to type; The Voice and V.O. act as if her movie)

THE VOICE:
"His tormented body rolled not in brine but in blood, which bubbled and seethed ... Jet after jet of white smoke was shot from the spiracle of the whale. ... Hauling in upon his crooked lance, Stubb straightened it again and again, then again and again sent it into the whale ... " [4]

CHARLENE:
Jesus. I can't use that crap. Erase. "Cut to — "

V.O.
"CUT TO: FLASHBACK. EXTERIOR. THE BOY, in the bushes, watches THE WOMAN smoke. His tongue gently flicks his own lips in response.

(We see Clyde at the picture window, easing himself against the sliding glass window, watching Charlene)

"CUT TO: INTERIOR. THE WOMAN, in front of the mirror, oblivious to being watched. She arches her throat and releases a jet of smoke."

(Clyde at the window disappears.)

"CUT TO: EXTERIOR. Now we see THE BOY begin to manipulate himself with the gloved hand.

CUT TO: INTERIOR. THE WOMAN hears a noise, and turns to the window.

CUT TO: THE BOY begins to grow urgent in his need, and begins pounding the cupped glove — "

(There is a pounding at the door; Charlene is puzzled:)

Pounding, pounding the cupped glove —

(The pounding at the door grows louder)

CHARLENE:
(with some fear)
Who is that?

CLYDE:
(offstage)
Special Delivery! I got a package for you, Charlene —

CHARLENE:
CLYDE?!! Goddamn you — I'm calling the police —

(Charlene races to her trimline on the desk; she dials 911 but we hear nothing but clicks.)

CHARLENE:
Shit! What did you do to the phone?

CLYDE:
(offstage)
You don't need the phone, baby. I'm here to reach out and touch someone —

CHARLENE:
Goddamn! You're drunk again, aren't you? Get away from here, Clyde! I told that stupid-ass judge a restraining order wouldn't work —

CLYDE:
(Pounding; offstage)
Open the fuckin' door. Now. I wanta talk to you.

(Charlene, with a grim calm, reaches into the desk drawer and pulls out a gun. She checks the ammo. we hear a click-possibly amplified.)

CHARLENE:
I'm working.

CLYDE:
I asked! Nicely!

(we hear the door being violently kicked. Charlene sits back down at her computer, and waits.

V.O.
(Urgently)
"CUT TO: EXTERIOR. THE BOY thrusts
himself against the front door
CUT TO: INTERIOR. THE WOMAN, on the
other side of the door, presses against it —

CLYDE:
(offstage)
— I'm Coming! I'm Coming in —
(With another savage kick, the door flies open.)
CLYDE:
Shit!!
(Clyde flies in, disheveled, drunk. Clyde grins, sings)
CLYDE:
"I hear you KNOCKIN' But You Can't Come In!"
CHARLENE:
Get out of here, Clyde. Your last chance.
(Charlene pretends to type.)
CLYDE:
I'm here to audition. To Give You. New Material. The E-Rot-icly
UnEmployed. To get your undivided attention. Write this up,
Baby. Oh my god! Is that a doorknob in my pocket or am I just
happy to see you? Baby? Stop looking at the goddamn screen.
Look. At. me.
(Before Charlene can stop him, Clyde pulls the computer plug
from the outlet.)
Ta-DA! And Now! The Burlesque Theatre of Langley Park!
Presentin'! SEX — ON — WELFARE!
(Clyde begins to strip and grind, taking off his T-shirt, and unzip-
ping his dungarees, while singing the trumpet "stripper theme.")
"BWAH-BWAH-BWAH!!! BWAH-BWAH-BWAH-BWAHHH!!!
BWAH-BWAH-BWAH!! BWAH-BWAH-BWAH-BWAH-bwah-
BWAHH!! — bum-bum **BWAHH!!** — bum-bum **BWAHH** —
bum-bum **BWAHH** — bum-bum ... "
(At this point, he has turned his back on Charlene, and has lowered

his pants and underwear, mooning her. Charlene stands, calmly, with the gun in her hand.)

CHARLENE:

I want. you. to stand. Very Still. Don't move, Clyde. Don't.Move.
(Clyde, seeing the gun, stops, still bent over, exposed.)
I don't want to kill you. By accident. I'm just going to shoot you just enough to send you to the hospital.
(Clyde, panicked, begins to rush for the door.)

CLYDE:

Jesus Christ — Char-LENE!!

(**Red Lights On.** There is the sound of an amplified gun shot. Very slowly, in stylized motion, Clyde grabs his behind, and writhes, a slow, sexual grind of agony. A male porn star voice dictates:)

THE VOICE:

He was Hot. He was throbbing. He was Hot He was Throbbing. He was Hot He was throbbing He was hot and throbbing He was hot He was throbbing He was hot and throbbing He was hot He was throbbing he was hot and throbbing He was hot He was throbbing —
(Charlene hides the gun. When the **regular lights** come up, Clyde is lying on his stomach on the sofa. Charlene, holding towels, stands over him. Clyde is crying.)

CLYDE:

Jesus H. Jesus H. Christ. I can't believe it. My own wife. I can't believe —

CHARLENE:

Hold still. Calm down and quit wiggling like that. I can't see anything with you moving around —

CLYDE:

Am I gonna haveta be in a wheelchair? For Life?

CHARLENE:

I said. hold. still. I don't want any blood on the carpeting.
(Charlene regards the wound. Charlene regards the Man's butt.)

CHARLENE:

Yup. I gotcha, all right. A flesh wound. How does it feel?

CLYDE:

How does it feel? How does it *feel?!* Like someone rammed a poker in my flesh! That's how it feels!

31

CHARLENE:
Don't move.

V.O.
— "Don't — "

THE VOICE:
— "Don't move." —

V.O.
(seductive whisper)
CUT TO: FLASHBACK — FIVE YEARS AGO.

(**Red Light** comes on. Clyde turns on his back, and Charlene straddles him. They begin to make out. The Voice turns into the Detective)
THE VOICE:
It's a Friday Night. And it's the first heat wave in the nation's capital. The Politicians are dying to leave town. Oh yeah — And it's a full moon. There's just two things to do on a night like this: make like cats in heat under the AC on high, or shoot somebody. And so the crime index climbs as high as the humidity. The waiting's the worst part. 'Cause I'm the dumb sucker who turns up first on the scene, and then waits around until the lab guys show up with their samples and body bags to clean up the mess

V.O.
(Back to her screenplay/dominatrix voice)
"CUT TO: — "

(Abrupt **lighting change:** back to bright stage light. Charlene stands over Clyde, now on his stomach again, with bandages, tape and antiseptic.)
CHARLENE:
I said Don't Move! You're gonna mess up my sofa! Thank God for Scotchguard … There. That's better. You might not need stitches.
THE VOICE:(Reading)
"Tha's got such a nice tail on thee. Tha's got the nicest arse of

anybody." [5]

(Charlene pours on liquid from the bottle; Clyde roars.)

CLYDE:

AAHHH!!

CHARLENE:

It's a Flesh Wound! It's not supposed to sting like that —

CLYDE:

Don't. You. Tell. Me. How It Feels! You Ain't My Butt!!

CHARLENE:

I can't do anything with you when you get in moods like this.

(Charlene efficiently bandages him; tears the tape with her teeth. She whiffs the air.)

CHARLENE:

Hooey! God, Clyde. You can't afford ta buy yourself bvd's, but you can throw it away on alcohol.

CLYDE:

It's my money.

CHARLENE:

I'm getting you some coffee before we go to the hospital. Sit up slowly. And sit on the towel.

(Like a man missing a limb, Clyde tentatively feels his behind. Slowly, he pulls up his underwear. He tries to pull up his jeans, winces, and leaves himself undone. He sits up penitently, like a little boy, on the towel, favoring his good cheek.

(offstage)

There's no milk in the house! So you haveta drink it black!

(**Red Light.** while the Voice speaks, Clyde slowly reaches into the back of his pants, wetting his hand with the blood. Hypnotically, he stares at the red on his hand, either getting faint or aroused. Clyde closes his eyes, bringing his hand closer to his face. He breathes in the scent of the blood, and then almost tastes his hand. He wipes his hand on the sofa.)

THE VOICE:

What the TV dramas don't show you is that we spend most of our days sitting on our butts, drinking stale coffee. And when we do get to the crime scene, the trails and traces are so stupid a kid could tell you who done it. And the action has come and gone long before you turned up. And so you feel like one big limp dick. That's why some of the guys round up the usual suspects who didn't do it, take 'em downtown, and backhand them — to feel some warm flesh on your flesh, the hot blood on the back of your hand — because a crime scene is a cold, cold place.

(The Voice commands:)

Jump Cut!

(Charlene hands coffee to Clyde)

CHARLENE:
Jesus! How did you get blood all over?

CLYDE:
I guess I sprayed a bit when ... the shot ... hit me.

CHARLENE:
Drink this. Slowly. Then we'll go.

CLYDE:
Okay.

(Clyde and Charlene sit at opposite ends of the sofa, sipping their coffee.)

CLYDE:
Good coffee.

(Charlene looks suspiciously at him.)

So — this is like old times, huh? Us sitting up, drinking coffee —

CHARLENE:
Forget it, Clyde. Whatever you're thinking, forget it.

THE VOICE:
CUT! Take two.

CLYDE:
So this is like old times, huh. Us sitting up, drinking coffee —

CHARLENE:
Forget it, Clyde. Whatever you're thinking, forget it.

(Pause.)

How does it feel?

CLYDE:
The more coffee I drink, the more it throbs.

THE VOICE:
I want you to —

CHARLENE:
"I want you to *feel* it. Maybe then you'll — "

THE VOICE: — *listen.*"

(Charlene just hears what she has said.)
CHARLENE:
Jesus. That sounds like something you would say.
(Pause.)
CLYDE:
Say, uh, what happened to the — ?
CHARLENE:
Don't worry about the gun. Just behave yourself, and it won't go off.
CLYDE:
Call me old-fashioned but I prefer the days when havin' protection
in the house meant your supply of birth control.
CHARLENE:
You're a laugh riot tonight.
CLYDE:
Seriously, Charlene, I don't like to think about you havin' guns 'n'
shit in the house —
CHARLENE:
It's my house.
(Clyde stands with some pain.)
CHARLENE:
Where are you going?
CLYDE:
I can't talk to you when you're like this.
THE VOICE:
CUT! Take three.
CLYDE:
I came to talk and you're shutting me out.
CHARLENE:
You're about ten years too late.
THE VOICE:
Jump Cut!
CLYDE:
So. How's work?
CHARLENE:
I'm behind deadline.
CLYDE:
How are ... the "gals?" At work?

CHARLENE:
The women?

CLYDE:
Right. Are you starting to turn a profit at — ? I don't remember the name of your production company.

CHARLENE:
Gyno Productions.

CLYDE:
Right. I knew it rhymed with wino. I never can remember it.

CHARLENE:
It's the root for "woman." In Greek.

CLYDE:
I can see that's important. But it's still hard to remember.

CHARLENE:
Yeah. It is. But we just designed a new logo, for our stationery and business cards — want to see it?

CLYDE:
Sure.

(Charlene goes to her desk, opens the middle drawer and takes out a business card which she gives to Clyde.)

CLYDE:
Wow. Charlene Dwyer. Story Editor, Gyno Productions. They promoted you. That's really nice, Charlene.

CHARLENE:
No, not that — what do you think of our new mascot?

CLYDE:
Well, I'm not sure — what is that thing on here? What is it doin' — it's dancing?

CHARLENE:
It's a Rhinoceros — "Rosie the Rhino." She's dancing.

CLYDE:
Uh-huh. That's cute. But, don't you. think. Those pink ... pasties ... are goin, a bit far?

(Clyde looks closer)

And the G-String? A Rhino in a G-string does not inspire me.

CHARLENE:
I like the G-string. It was my idea. And it's supposed to be ... funny. For women.

(beat)

Are you done with your coffee?

CLYDE:

Look, do you want to talk? Talking involves disagreement. If I
don't tell you what I'm thinking, even if it's ignorant, how can I
learn anything about what you're doing when you say you're
working.

CHARLENE:

Yeah? Like What do you want to know?

CLYDE:

Well — do you ever think you're gonna run out of words when
you're writing like that?

V.O.

She thinks about it all the time.

(Charlene stares at Clyde)

CHARLENE:

I think about it all the time.

(beat)

Can I have my business card back, please?

CLYDE:

I'd like to keep it, if I may. As a ... memento. I know it has ... your
work number on it — but I won't use it. Okay?

CHARLENE:

Right.

V.O.

Shit, that was dumb, Charlene.

(Charlene sits, tensely)

CLYDE:

Just relax, will ya? So where do all these words come from?

CHARLENE:

I don't know. When I really get going, it's like a trance — it's not me
writing at all. It's as if I just listen to voices and I'm taking dictation.

THE VOICE:

Sometimes when I'm waiting for the body bags, I'll look at the victims. Sometimes they're real pretty. And I'll think — she's young enough to be my daughter, or maybe she's someone's mother — it makes it hard to go home. And sometimes I talk to them ... and their voices answer me. I mean, I know it's me, but ... mostly I say I'm sorry. And they tell me it's all right. Frankly, it scares the shit out of me.

CLYDE:
Doesn't that spook you? I mean, whose voices are these? Who's in control?

V.O.
But she was in control.
(The Voice and V.O. begin to make out behind the sofa.)

CHARLENE:
Well, they're the characters speaking. They kindof ... sit in the living room and talk to me. I mean, I know it's me, but I have to get into it. Right now I'm writing something with this detective who goes to investigate a homicide and he meets a woman. And there's this incredible physical attraction that happens at the crime scene. (The Voice and Voice-Over start to make out behind the sofa.)

CLYDE:
Uh-huh. I used to think that porno flicks were all pictures and no words —

CHARLENE:
Look, Clyde, I don't write *porno*. I didn't appreciate you telling Leslie Ann that.

CLYDE:
Well, what do you call it? What was the title of your last opus? *Sperms of Endearment?!* So what is that — Bergman?

CHARLENE:
It's my homage to Jack Nicholson.

CLYDE:
Uh-huh.

CHARLENE:
Gyno Productions is a feminist film company dedicated to producing women's erotica.

CLYDE:
Erotica is just a Swedish word for porn, Charlene.
CHARLENE:
What's the use? Are you through with your coffee?
CLYDE:
Look, this is what happens every time I challenge you. You just.shut.down. As if I'm bullying you. And it's just my way. It's the way men learn to argue through contact sports. As if words were body grease, so you gotta grab hard to pin your opponent. And I'm stuck here, feeling stupid and cut off, because you won't explain things in plain English. You speak in a code. A code designed for signals between members of the female sex. Well, pardon me, but I did.not.go.to.college.

V.O.
He's.An.Asshole.

CHARLENE:
In plain English: I am not a pornographer. I write erotic enter-tainment designed for women.
CLYDE:
Yeah. So to return to what I was askin': what's the big difference? (The Voice and Voice-Over begin to make orgiastic noises when Charlene says "aroused.")
CHARLENE:
For one thing, desire in female spectators is aroused by cinema in a much different way. Narrativity — that is, plot — is emphasized.
CLYDE:
(stares at her)
Yeah. There are lots more words. So what else?
CHARLENE:
The "meat shots" and "money shots" of the trade flicks are not the be-all and end-all of Gyno Productions. — why are you laughing?
CLYDE:
I seen one of your movies — and it had tits and ass just like DEEP THROAT.
CHARLENE:
Physical expression is the culmination of relationships between

characters. Most importantly, we try to create women as protagonists in their own dramas, rather than objects. And we try to appreciate the male body as an object of desire.

CLYDE:
Now you're talking!
(in his enthusiasm, Clyde moves too much and flinches.)
— Oh, suffering Jesus on the cross!

CHARLENE:
Is it bad?

CLYDE:
Yeah.

V.O.
Awww.

CHARLENE:
Come on, let's go —

CLYDE:
No, wait a minute, wait a second. I'm a ... little woozy. Do you have anything in the house. For the pain?

CHARLENE:
Whatd'ya mean, for the pain?

CLYDE:
I could use a shot of something.

CHARLENE:
You want me to give you a drink, Clyde? Are you insane?

CLYDE:
One drink is not gonna hurt. In fact, it will dull the throbbing in my butt. And since it is your bullet that's in my butt, I think you owe me. One.

CHARLENE:
You get mean when you drink. I don't want to participate in enabling behavior.

CLYDE:
Goddamn Oprah Winfrey! Just get me something, will ya, Charlene? My Butt is bitchin ...

CHARLENE:
One Shot. That's all. I'll get some for me.

(Charlene exits. While she is out of the room, Clyde quickly searches under the sofa pillows and cushions for the gun. She returns with a bottle and two shot glasses. Charlene pours them drinks and hands Clyde his glass.)

CLYDE:
Wow. That's nice.

CHARLENE:
It's Remy.

CLYDE:
It's been a while ... since I had Remy. Well — let's toast. To love and success and a long film career — to you.

CHARLENE:
To ... to you. To you, Clyde.
(They sip. Pause.)

THE VOICE:
Jump Cut!

CHARLENE:
You've got to let go now. It's over.

CLYDE:
I ... kinda lost my head when I got that restraining order today, Charlene. Some things will never be *over.* Like everything you taught me.

CHARLENE:
What did I teach you?

CLYDE:
You taught me about desire. That's not over. I think about you all the time. I have since high school.

CHARLENE:
You're not thinking about me — you're obsessing about me.

CLYDE:
No — because you can never understand what's going on inside a man's head, you imagine the worst.

V.O.
Charlene. Get him out of the house.

THE VOICE:
Jump Cut!

41

CLYDE:
I'm gonna put myself together — get retrained in something. Maybe go back to school like you did. It really changed you, Charlene, when you went back to school.
CHARLENE:
I think that would be wonderful.
CLYDE:
I have to work out my "karma." Because I really fucked it up in this lifetime. And I have to pay for that by trying.
CHARLENE:
I don't believe in "karma."
CLYDE:
I do. I believe in it. There's no other way to explain stuff like high school proms ...
(Charlene laughs, relaxes. Clyde smiles, and moves a little closer)
CHARLENE:
I forget sometimes how unique you are. When you're not drinking.
THE VOICE:
(reading)
"She will embrace me warmly, as if we had never embraced before. We will have only a couple of hours together and then she will leave — to go to work. I will be sound asleep when she returns at three or four in the morning ... I love her, heart and soul. She is everything to me." [6]
CLYDE:
You're everything to me.
(Charlene pours another round of Remy)

V.O.
You've had enough for one night, Charlene.

THE VOICE:
Jump Cut!
CHARLENE:
I ... think about you. I try to figure it out. All the time. Why I stayed with it so long. It's funny — I always asked why I stayed — I never thought to ask how you could act that way. And then one

day, I realized that every dish in the house had been replaced with plastic ones. Part of me got off, living on the edge like that. I kept saying, I can handle this, I can take this — but I was losing control.

THE VOICE:
Jump Cut!

CLYDE:
I never stop thinking about it. It's this tape loop. It's torturing me. I'm standing outside my body, watching this actor doing that to you. A stunt man who's got my face.

THE VOICE:
(reading)
"She loved me for the dangers I had passed.
And I loved her that she did pity them." [7]

CHARLENE:
You want to work out your karma? Then let go. Find another woman, and make her life lucky. Break the cycle. It will be better, the next time.

V.O.
"She can … smell … his sweat. So warm, she can smell — "

THE VOICE:
"So close, she can almost taste — "

V.O.
"Smell. His. — "

THE VOICE:
"Sweat."
(A **red light** fills the stage again. There is a rustling at the sliding glass window. We see Calvin against the glass, watching. He stretches his arms against the frame.)

CLYDE:
It will never be as good as it is with you.

THE VOICE:
"CUT TO: INTERIOR. THE WOMAN closes her eyes."
(Charlene closes her eyes.)

THE VOICE:
"CLOSE UP on her lips as she kisses THE MAN, hard, on the mouth."
(Charlene sits by Clyde and gently kisses him. They look at each other. Then they kiss again — a long, hard kiss, breathing each other in.)

V.O.
"What are you doing, Charlene?"

THE VOICE:
"THE MAN and THE WOMAN look at each other for a long time."

V.O.
"This is not a movie, Charlene."

THE VOICE:
"THE MAN and THE WOMAN move toward each other, lips parted."

V.O.
(Urgent)
"CUT TO: EXTERIOR. we see the door of the house burst open and — "

THE VOICE:
(Cutting in)
— "THE WOMAN begins to breathe, quicker; THE MAN moves closer and presses against her, urgent now — "

V.O.
(Trying harder)
"CUT TO — CUT TO: EXTERIOR! we see THE WOMAN run from the house — "

THE VOICE:
"THE WOMAN sighs; THE MAN reaches out and strokes

her hair — "

THE VOICE:
"LONG SHOT. EXTERIOR. THE BOY watches through the
window."
(There is a freeze. Clyde and Charlene on the sofa; Calvin,
stretched on the window. The **red light** changes to the **stage
lights.** Clyde starts unbuttoning Charlene's top.)
CHARLENE:
What about your — ? — No, wait
CLYDE:
Shhh! Don't Talk. Not now.
(Clyde and Charlene resume. Just then the door flies open violently;
Calvin flies into the room.)
CALVIN:
I AM. GONNA. *KILL* YOU!!
CLYDE:
What the fuck — ?
(In a fury, Calvin throws himself on top of the couple. Clyde and
Calvin roll onto the floor. Clyde screams.)
CLYDE:
SHIT! AAAAH!
CHARLENE:
CALVIN! NO! STOP! Watch out for his butt!
(Clyde and Calvin wrestle. They stand. Calvin, from behind, gets
Clyde in a lock, one hand pinned and twisted; Calvin's arm is
locked around Clyde's throat, choking him.)
CLYDE:
(In a squeezed voice:)
It's getting harder to ... be a ... family man ... these days.
CALVIN:
You leave her alone. Understand?
CHARLENE:
Calvin. It's not. As it looks.

CALVIN:
You don't live here anymore. Get it?
CLYDE:
(Appreciatively, in the same squeezed voice)
You're getting … Mighty big, son.
(And just as quickly, Clyde slips around and out of Calvin's grip, quickly kneeing him in the groin. Calvin gasps and falls into a fetal position on the rug.)
CHARLENE:
Jesus Christ, Clyde!
CLYDE:
He's playing with the big boys now.
(Calvin says nothing. His face, beet red, presses into the rug.)
CHARLENE:
Calvin —
CLYDE:
Don't touch him. He'll be all right.
(Pause)
Son? You all right?
(Clyde offers his hand to Calvin, who refuses it, and who slowly gets up.)
CLYDE:
I'm sorry. Reflex action. No man likes to injure the family jewels.
CHARLENE:
Calvin —
CALVIN:
What's he doin' here?
CHARLENE:
Your father … just …
CLYDE:
Dropped in. For a little adult conversation.
CALVIN:
That's not what it looked like to me.
CHARLENE:
Honey, I can appreciate your concern, but he's still your father —
CALVIN:
What's he doin' here?

CLYDE:
Look, maybe I should just call it a night.

CHARLENE:
No, wait a minute, Clyde. No matter what's happened between you and me, you and Calvin have to learn how to talk to one another. I will not be used as an excuse for getting in the middle of the two of you. Do you both hear me? I want you to both act civilized to each other in my living room for at least sixty seconds.
(Beat)
I'm putting on a fresh pot of coffee.
(Charlene exits)

CLYDE:
Whatta night, huh?
(As Clyde hobbles past Calvin to sit on the sofa.)

CALVIN:
Hey, what happened to your butt?

CLYDE:
Your poor, defenseless mother shot me.

CALVIN:
Mom? Mom? She Shot you?
(Calvin starts to laugh)

CLYDE:
I don't see anything particularly amusing about it. Men might hit you in the balls, but they do it to your face. Women — they shoot you in the butt.

CALVIN:
You musta deserved it.

CLYDE:
This is something private between your mother and me.
(Pause)
So — how's school?

CALVIN:
Okay.

CLYDE:
And life? In general.

CALVIN:
Okay.

CLYDE:
Still got your nose stuck in the books? Instead of watchin' the live action?

CALVIN:
Real men can read books.

CLYDE:
Right, right.
(Another Pause)

CLYDE:
So — how's your sister?

CALVIN:
Okay, I guess.

CLYDE:
You guess? You don't know? You gotta keep an eye on her, son. She's at ... that age. Know what I mean?
(Clyde punches Calvin in his arm. Calvin rubs his arm.)

CALVIN:
Yeah, sure I do.

CLYDE:
That's right. You're the man of the house, now. Blood of my blood, flesh of my flesh. Best thing to do is just lock her up for a couple a years. She's gonna cause a lot of men heartbreak. You gotta watch her, son.

CALVIN:
I do. I watch her all the time.

CLYDE:
I mean, it's not her fault, right? But that body of hers ... you know what I mean? You got to control her.

CALVIN:
She's a little hard to control.

CLYDE:
Girls' bodies at her age ... they should be *licensed*.
(**Red light** stage left of glass door. Voice-Over begins to work to the music. Leslie Ann watches her work, shyly. Clyde and Calvin enjoy the show.)

CLYDE:
Where is ... your sister?

CALVIN:
She said she was goin' to some sleepover.
CLYDE:
And your mother believes that crap? We don't believe that crap, do we? (The two share a laugh, settle back and watch with glazed attention)
THE VOICE:
"One of the little things that made Cleo's dance fascinating was the little pompom she wore in the center ... it served to keep your eyes riveted to the spot. She could rotate it like a pinwheel or make it jump and quiver with little electric spasms."
(Leslie Ann starts to join in from her spot, hesitantly at first. Clyde hands his son a dollar bill, and shows him how to offer it to the Voice-Over)
"Sometimes it would subside with little gasps, like a swan coming to rest ... it seemed to be a part of her. it was tantalizing, especially to the sixteen year old who had still to know what it feels like to make a grab for a woman's bush." [8]
(**Red Lights** out. Voice-Over goes back upstage, and Leslie Ann disappears. Charlene enters with a tray, a coffee pot, two mugs, a plate of cookies. And a tall glass of milk. Charlene pauses, watches them. She sets the tray clown on the coffee table.)
CHARLENE:
You two are just ... chattering away like magpies.
CLYDE:
We've been talking. Right?
CALVIN:
Yup.
CLYDE:
Man talk.
CALVIN:
You just caught us during the pause.
CHARLENE:
I've fixed us a late-night snack. A last cup of coffee before I drive your father to the hospital.
CLYDE:
I don't think that's ... necessary, Charlene.

CHARLENE:
This is nothing to fool around with, Clyde. Let me see how it's doing. Turn over.
CLYDE:
Not in front of the boy, goddamn it.
CHARLENE:
For Christ's sake, he's your own flesh and blood. Turn over.
(Clyde turns his wounded cheek toward her. She carefully lowers his pants and examines the wound critically. Calvin peeks.)
CALVIN:
Wow.
CHARLENE:
It's still bleeding. Not as bad as before, though. It needs stitches and a fresh bandage.
(Pause.)
CALVIN:
Mom? Didja really shoot Dad?
CHARLENE:
Yes.
CALVIN:
Cool. Mom?
CHARLENE:
Calvin, we're not going to discuss it.
CLYDE:
Why don't you just drink up your milk and go to bed ...
(Calvin stares with disbelief and disgust at the glass of milk.)
CALVIN:
You have got to be shittin' me ...
CLYDE:
Lucky for you this is your mother's house. I'd turn the strap on ya for language like that ...
CALVIN:
Mom! Milk?!! MILK!?
CHARLENE:
Well, sweetie, it's too late for you to be drinking coffee, and I saved the last glass of milk to go with your cookies.
CALVIN:
I'm not drinking that shit.

CLYDE:
Growing boys need their milk. Right?

CHARLENE:
Let's just drop it, Clyde.

CLYDE:
Only wusses are scared of milk. A real man can drink milk.

CALVIN:
You drink it.

CLYDE:
Okay, son — I'll show you how it's done. How a real man drinks milk —

CHARLENE:
Stop it. Stop it. I hate this.
(Clyde abruptly grabs the milk, and guzzles half the glass. It dribbles down his chin and shirt.)

CLYDE:
Num, num. A man who can't drink milk can't love women. Is that a problem for you, son? Are you that kind of man?

CHARLENE:
Why does everything turn into a horror movie around here?

CLYDE:
Show your old man. Drink the milk.
(Clyde presses the glass into Calvin's face. They freeze.)

THE VOICE:
"There the mark of his teeth still where he tried to bite the nipple. I had to scream out aren't they fearful trying to hurt you — " [9]
(End freeze)

CLYDE:
Drink the milk.

CALVIN:
No. Shit! Get out of my face.

CLYDE:
It's just Milk. What are you scared of? Milk can't hurt you — (The two tussle with the milk; it splashes them both.)

CALVIN:
You're. An. Asshole!
(Charlene and Calvin instinctively flinch. A moment's pause.)

CLYDE:
(quietly)
What.did.you.call.me?
CHARLENE:
— Enough!
(Calvin goes to Charlene, scared.)
CALVIN:
You don't scare me. This is not your house. You keep away from us. Stop thrusting yourself on Mom, You.Hear.Me?
CLYDE:
I wasn't thrusting myself on your mother. Quite the opposite. Did I thrust myself on you on the sofa, Charlene? Did I?
CHARLENE:
I'm taking you to the hospital. Now.
CLYDE:
Your mother kissed me. First.

CHARLENE	**CALVIN**
(together with Calvin)	(with Charlene)
— This is getting ridiculous —	— That's a lie! isn't it, mom?

CHARLENE:
We're ending this conversation. Now.
CLYDE:
Tell him. You kissed me.
CALVIN:
Don't be scared of him, Mom. I'm here.
CLYDE:
I know it's hard to believe, Calvin. She's amazing when she kisses —
CALVIN:
Did.You.Kiss.Him? Mom? After all he's done?
THE VOICE:
"and his heart was going like mad and yes I said yes I — " [10]
CHARLENE:
Calvin — honey — it's hard to explain, at your age — it was just … for old time's sake!
CALVIN:
I DON'T BELIEVE YOU!
CLYDE:
Don't raise your voice like that to your mother —

CHARLENE:
For God's sake, Calvin, I'm a human being, too — I have needs —
CALVIN:
I'm Getting Out.Of.Here —
CLYDE:
When your mother kisses a man, it's like your heart gets squeezed.
Too bad she's your mother and you'll never know —
CALVIN:
ARGGHHH!!
(Holding his head, Calvin rushes for the door, opens it and runs
out into the night, screaming:)
I AM SO FUCKED UP!
(Door slam)
THE VOICE:
"She kissed me. I was kissed. All yielding she tossed my hair.
 Kissed, she kissed me.
  Me. And me now." [11]
(Clyde and Charlene sit, weary and tense.)
CHARLENE:
Why do you always do that?
CLYDE:
Do what?
CHARLENE:
Oh, you know. You know very well.
CLYDE:
(getting angry)
Christ!
(Clyde and Charlene look at each other. **Red Light**)

V.O.
FLASHBACK — THREE YEARS AGO.
(Clyde strikes Charlene hard on the face; in slow motion, it almost
looks like a caress. Charlene falls back on the sofa. Clyde continues
toward Charlene:)
"CUT TO — "

(Abrupt lighting change: back to bright **stage lights**. Charlene
stands, scared.)

CHARLENE:
(trying to be composed)
Calm down.

CLYDE:
Calm down — I don't have a job, I've got no fuckin' family, no wife — I've got shit for a life!

CHARLENE:
Maybe you should go now.

THE VOICE:
"We will have only a couple of hours together and then she will leave — " 12

CLYDE:
Christ, Charlene. I just wish — shit, I just wish we could go back, ya know? Before college, before I got fired, before everything started busting apart. I wish I could just close my eyes and you'd be coming home through the door in your uniform, after your night shift.

CHARLENE:
Oh God, I hated that fucking uniform. It made my backside enormous.

CLYDE:
You'd come in, tired but sweet. I'm under the covers. First you flip on the coffee in the kitchen, and the aroma comes up to me before you reach the bed. And then I feel your hands on my stubble, stroking it, and then I hear the sound of your shoes hitting the floor, one by one. And the zippers. The sound of the uniform sliding down your slip. And then the next thing I know, there's your warmth in bed. And your voice urging me up to work. Already slipping into sleep.
And every morning I went to work with a hard-on. It was great.

CHARLENE:
Great.
(Charlene stares into nothing as she slowly pours the coffee as a trickle into a cup.)
And every night I would stand in the middle of the ward and think, I can't do this any longer." Holding another bed pan, swimming with someone's fluids. Bodies and mess. Mess and Bodies. Minimum wage. Cleaning up messes.

V.O.

This is where a high school diploma gets you,
Charlene.

CLYDE:
But then you came home. To me and the children.
CHARLENE:
Where I cleaned up your mess for free. Now I can close my eyes
and see beautiful, strong, bodies touching each other, coupling
with each other. And I write down these words. And the words
become flesh.
(Beat)
And the pay's much better, too.
CLYDE:
I could kill that little faculty fruit at P.G. Community —
CHARLENE:
Gil may not have been the world's most inspired creative writing
teacher, but he took pity on me — a woman with two kids to
support needing a way to pay the rent. He encouraged me; he let
me in on the market. This writing is saving my sanity. I'm never
going back.
(Pause)
CLYDE:
So where's Leslie Ann at tonight?
CHARLENE:
She's spending the night with a friend.
CLYDE:
A friend, huh.
CHARLENE:
Yes. A girlfriend. She asked my permission.
CLYDE:
It's your house.
CHARLENE:
Don't you dare start implying —
CLYDE:
What? Who? Who's implying — ?

CHARLENE:
I work very hard at being a good mother.

CLYDE:
You're a great mother.

CHARLENE:
I try, that's all.

CLYDE:
Leslie Ann's just at ... that age, is all. You know.

CHARLENE:
No, I don't know. What age is that?

CLYDE:
You can't be too careful. Look, I'm hardly the one to give you advice ... seeing how my backseat activities got me into messes.

CHARLENE:
I know exactly where my children are. I know exactly where Leslie Ann is, right now.

V.O.
"CUT TO: INTERIOR. in the rec room of Lisa's house. Night."

(On the ramp, Leslie Ann, now in an oversized T-shirt, huddles in her sleeping bag, addressing her best friend Lisa. Leslie Ann and Voice-Over speak to each other.)

LESLIE ANN:
You're my best friend, Lisa. You.know.that. Since Seventh Grade. And you're gonna be my best friend long after I get married and have kids. If it wasn't for the fact.that.I get to see you for home-room and lunch, I woulda stopped goin' to that stupid school a long time ago.

V.O.
Uh.huh. Is your sleeping bag warm enough?

LESLIE ANN:
I feel like there's nothin' you couldn't tell me. You know? I would die before one'a your secrets would roll out.of.my.mouth.

V.O.
Me too. You could tell me — anything.

LESLIE ANN:
That's good. Are the other girls ... asleep? ... Do you — do. you —

V.O.
What? Come on, you can tell me anything —

LESLIE ANN:
I've never said this to anyone else before. I'll kill you if you —

V.O.
— You can tell me. Anything.

LESLIE ANN:
Well. Do you ... do you ... think of boys a lot?

V.O.
(Giggling)
All the time.

LESLIE ANN:
But I mean do you think about ... think about ...

V.O.
What? What? About ... doing it?

LESLIE ANN:
Yeah, but not just that —
(In a rush)
I mean, I think of that, too, but sometimes ... do you think of
them, like, "hurting" you? Well, I don't mean like hurting you, but
like, you're tied down and you can't stop them and they do things
to you that hurt you, that make you scream but you can't and you
wouldn't really want it to happen in real life, you would really get
hurt, but when you close your eyes, you see it and it makes you get
hot only it's 'cause it's not for real?

(Pause)

Lisa? Lisa? Are you asleep?

(The Voice claps a Film slate. **Lights** back up on living room.)

CHARLENE:

Leslie Ann is still a child. And I want her to have every second of childhood that she can get.

CLYDE:

A child, huh? Have you looked at your daughter lately?

CHARLENE:

There's too much pressure on her, already. Lectures on safe sex, birth control, condoms … I want.her.left.alone.

CLYDE:

Okay, okay. You're her mother. But have you walked out of your front door lately: Seen the world? There's no childhood left.

CHARLENE:

It's not the world outside I'm worried about her seeing.

CLYDE:

What's that supposed to mean?

(Pause)

CHARLENE:

I think we should go now. I'll drive you.

CLYDE:

I can drive myself.

CHARLENE:

Let's go, then.

CLYDE:

I'm not ready.

THE VOICE:

Cut! Take two.

CHARLENE:

It's late. I want you out of here.

CLYDE:

I just got here.

CHARLENE:

Don't.

CLYDE:

What am I doing? Having a cup of coffee?

CHARLENE:
You can't stay, Clyde. I need you out of here.
THE VOICE:
Cut! Take three.
CHARLENE:
I want you out of here.
CLYDE:
Are you going to make me?
CHARLENE:
If I have to.
CLYDE:
Ooooh.
CHARLENE:
Don't mock me, goddamn you —
(There is the sound of door keys, loud heavy metal music and a door slam. Leslie Ann enters. They all blink at each other.)
CLYDE:
Hi, baby girl.
LESLIE ANN:
Daddy!
(To Charlene)
You didn't tell me he was gonna be here.
CHARLENE:
What are you doing here?
LESLIE ANN:
I came back for somethin' — Lisa's waiting outside —
CHARLENE:
Why don't you just go back out to the car and Lisa —
LESLIE ANN:
— Why didn't you tell me my father was coming tonight?
CHARLENE:
Did you notice the knob is off the front door?
CLYDE:
Don't I get a kiss anymore?
(Leslie Ann runs to her father and hugs him.)
That's more like it. … My God, you're getting big. What you are you doing tonight, princess?

LESLIE ANN:
I'm doin' a sleepover at Lisa's — she's my friend in the car. Do you want to meet her?
CLYDE:
No — that's okay. What do you girls do together?
LESLIE ANN:
We're watching movies, mostly. *Friday the 13th, Halloween* —

V.O.
(A la horror movie)
"Get out of the house! Get out of the — " [13]

CHARLENE:
I don't know how you can watch those.
LESLIE ANN:
They're just movies, mom.
(To Clyde)
Are you coming back home?
CHARLENE:
No! He was just leaving — we were on our way out —
LESLIE ANN:
I just got here!
CHARLENE:
Leslie Ann, your father and I are in the middle of something —
LESLIE ANN:
— Lay-la. Where's Calvin?
CLYDE:
He left after a little chat.
LESLIE ANN:
Are you gonna be here when I get back?
CHARLENE:
No.
LESLIE ANN:
You just came over for a visit, Daddy?
CLYDE:
I wanted to try to talk to your mother, that's all.
(Clyde hands Leslie Ann five dollars.)

LESLIE ANN:
Good luck. She's hard to talk to.
CHARLENE:
Okay. That's enough. Go on with Lisa —

V.O.
(whispered)
Don't Go.

LESLIE ANN:
Why don't you two just try to talk it out? Daddy, you've got to give up drinking, that's all. And get another job. It's no big deal. I don't see why you two can't work it out.
CLYDE:
Well, I'd like that, Layla.
CHARLENE:
It's a little more complicated than that, honey.
LESLIE ANN:
I'm gonna tell Lisa to go on without me.
CHARLENE:
No. You are going. With Lisa. And have a nice time.
LESLIE ANN:
Everybody gets to talk to him but me!
(There is the sound of a car horn. Three times. "Lo-lit-ta.")
THE VOICE:
Daddy's Girl ...
(Leslie Ann goes to the door and yells.)
LESLIE ANN:
Go on without me, okay?!
(There is the sound of a car horn, again, with the Voice echoing.)
THE VOICE:
Daddy's Girl ...
LESLIE ANN:
I wanna stay here and talk.

V.O.
(whispered)
Don't Go.

CHARLENE:
Not tonight. I mean it.

LESLIE ANN:
I can't even talk to my own father!! Why can't we be like other families?

LESLIE ANN:
Don't I even get a chance? Where's my fucking 4-H Club! When did we ever say grace at the dinner table?! I'm a fucking statistic from a broken home! A goddamn teenage statistic without enough money for a fucking double feature at the mall who has to lie that my mother's a secretary and that my father's a secret agent so no one finds out I've got a pervo for a mother, a drunk for a father and a four-eyed geek for a brother who beats-off in his catcher's mitt! FUCK!

(Leslie Ann slams out of the house. Pause)

CHARLENE:
I'm not a mean woman. But I'm really going to enjoy watching her when she has children of her own.

CLYDE:
I don't remember talking to my mother like that.

CHARLENE:
The only reason Leslie Ann thinks the sun shits out of your ass is 'cause I've lied to her all these many years. She thinks I'm just … clumsy.

CLYDE:
Yeah, well you are.

CHARLENE:
I wasn't "clumsy" until after we got married. Running into doors, falling down the stairs — I want to protect her from knowing. It's too late for Calvin. That last fight — he saw it.

CLYDE:
Part of becoming a man is accepting your parents' imperfections.

CHARLENE:
Imperfections, yes — broken ribs, no.

CLYDE:
Okay, Charlene. I've ruined your life. Okay? I'm fucked-up as a husband and a father, and I've ruined whatever fucking chance at happiness you and my children have in this lifetime.

CHARLENE:
I'm not asking you for that, Clyde.

CLYDE:
What do you want from me?

CHARLENE:
What do *I* want? Why'd you come over?

CLYDE:
I ... wanted to see you.

CHARLENE:
Why? What is it you want?

CLYDE:
I want ... I want ... what's the use.
(Clyde gets up to go.)

CHARLENE:
Just tell me the truth. Okay? I'm listening.

CLYDE:
You'll hate me if you know ...

CHARLENE:
I can't hate you more than I have for the past ten years.

CLYDE:
Well. Okay, this is hard for me, all right? It's ... it's a fuckin' Friday night. Right?
And so what do we do, Friday night? Go out, drink some beer, and ... ya know ... cruise the strip. I mean, if you're a guy who's alone, that's what there is to do in this town on a Friday.

CHARLENE:
I'm with you so far.

CLYDE:
Right. So I ... take a shower, you know, spruce up a little bit. And I count out the change I have left. And it's not much. And that gets me a little depressed, but I think, okay, shit, I'll economize, I'll buy a six-pack for the truck, and I won't drink out, you know? So I go downtown, and hit the streets ... and I go into a few ... places ... but mostly there are minimums. So I think, fuck, I can't even watch the live action.

CHARLENE:
You gotta have money to be a player.

CLYDE:
So ... so ... so I go into a corner bookstore, and it's packed. And I change a five into quarters, and slip into the booth ... and I —
CHARLENE:
— You watch —
CLYDE:
Right. And all it does is get me even more agitated. I'm thinking, this is not what I want, on A Friday Night, the feeling of my own fist in a booth — I'm like numb to that by now — and so I get back into my own truck, and I drink a few beers to get my nerve up — and I empty out my pockets ... I check the dash and under the seats, and I count — and I come up with a lousy eighteen dollars and thirty-seven cents.
CHARLENE:
Well, that's better than nothing.
CLYDE:
Are you being ... funny?
CHARLENE:
(quickly)
No, I'm not. ... Go on.
CLYDE:
Well, I think you know, times are hard, maybe some working girl will consider it — you know? Maybe I'll get lucky, or I'll hit someone green on the street — So I crank up the engine, and start to drive it slow, down the side streets. And I see them, it's warm out tonight, and they're there, in groups — laughing, wearing next to nothing, and they're so close, they're laughing at me, calling out to me —
CHARLENE:
— So why didn't you ask someone?
CLYDE:
— I don't know. They were all together. I couldn't get one off by herself; I thought they'd laugh — I couldn't just call out, you know, "How about $18.37?" I just ... just lost my nerve, I was so ... down by then ... then ... and then I just kept driving and the truck kind of drove here by itself.
CHARLENE:
(quietly)

So you're telling me that you drove to your ex-wife's house because you couldn't afford a prostitute.

CLYDE:

Jesus, Charlene, don't make it sound like that!

CHARLENE:

I'm not taking offense, Clyde. I'm a grown woman. I can take the truth. In fact, I prefer it.

CLYDE:

I mean, the truth is ... the truth is ... that lately nothing really seems to do it for me. I don't know what ... what's happening to me ... but all the usual ... uh ... escapes ... turn me on but they don't work anymore — I just get more and more depressed and anxious — like what if it just won't work at all, I mean, it happens, sometimes to men, and something's happening in ... in my head — well, frankly, it scares the shit out of me. And it's building into a big problem now.

CHARLENE:

I don't understand.

(Clyde starts to shake, ever so slightly, trying not to cry.)

CLYDE:

I mean like magazines, or girls in the booth, you know? I'll try to watch them, to use them but ... something's changed ... I start thinking, she's young enough to be my daughter, or ... I'll bet she's married, or she's someone's mother ... the words I read in the books I buy, I start to wonder if some woman's writing them, the way you do, to pay the rent for her kids ... and ... I think I'm really, really fucked-up. I'm sorry — I don't mean to do this to you, I know you've got problems of your own, but I just miss — just talking to you — you know?

(Clyde is crying, quietly, openly.)

CHARLENE:

(softly)

Oh My God, what have we done to each other.

(Charlene pats the sofa beside her)

CHARLENE:

Sit down. Just ... sit down. Okay?

(Pause. They sit quietly beside each other on the sofa. Charlene makes a decision.)

CHARLENE:
How are you feeling? Does it still hurt?
CLYDE:
Huh? Oh, that — no, I barely feel it. I think it's stopped bleeding.
CHARLENE:
Okay — listen. I'm just a woman on a Friday night, okay? I've come down on my price for you — just once — just for tonight — for $18.37. You've hit the jackpot, mister. I am not your wife — or anyone's mother right now. Just this once, Clyde — we've got to be quick, before the kids come back. Put the chain on the door, and make the sofa bed up, okay? The sheets are already on it, you've just got to take the cushions off and pull it out. I'm going ... to change into something.
(Clyde has a hard time talking)
CLYDE:
You don't have to ...
CHARLENE:
I know I don't.
CLYDE:
I'm not sure if I can ... if I —
CHARLENE:
Then we'll just hold each other and talk. All Right? Quick now, before I change my mind. I'll be right back.
(Charlene exits into the bathroom. Clyde, unable to believe his luck, sits for a few moments on the sofa. He notices the cognac bottle, picks it up and guzzles the cognac. Then slowly, he gets up, in pain. He draws the blinds closed. He begins to take the cushions off the sofa. When he turns his back to the audience, we can see that his jeans are soaked in blood. He sees that he has drenched the cushion, and quickly turns the bloody side to the wall.
Meanwhile, The Voice has become an actual detective. He examines the doorway, looking at the frame for signs of forced entry. He draws out a handkerchief, and finds a bullet casing on the floor. Using his handkerchief, he picks up and examines each glass and coffee cup, looking for prints, etc.)
CLYDE:
Charlene! Uh — Charlene — !

CHARLENE:
(offstage)
What!
CLYDE:
I don't have … anything on me … you know? In case —
CHARLENE:
(offstage)
That's okay. I've got some protection in the house.
(Laughs)
Not protection as in guns. Protection as in condoms. A girl scout
is always prepared …
(Clyde stops, Scowls. Angrier. **Red light** starts to blend in with the
stage lights, slowly. The detective finds a condom on the floor)
THE VOICE:
(as detective)
What is she doing with condoms in the house?

V.O.
And the words become flesh.
(Increasingly angry, Clyde begins to make up the bed. He sits
on the bed:)

CLYDE:
Ya know, Charlene — maybe if I go back to school, I'll try my
hand at screenplays!
CHARLENE:
(offstage)
What?
CLYDE:
I said, I could write some screenplays! 'Cause I've got all these
pictures — these voices — in my head, too …
(no answer from Charlene in the bathroom. To himself)
Yeah. I'd like to write a screenplay where the porno movie director
goes berserk in the middle of the movie, and strings up the bimbo
star and he fuckin' kills her, and then he tracks down the writer in
her living room …
Yeah …
(Clyde's screenplay starts to play. The Voice becomes a porn director)

67

THE VOICE:
Jump Cut!

> **V.O.**
> "She was hot. She was throbbing. But she was in control.
>
> Okay. Now we separate the men from the little boys …

THE VOICE:
— Cut! Listen, there's been a change in the script —

> **V.O.**
> What change?

THE VOICE:
Clyde says he wants the bondage in reverse. Okay?

> **V.O.**
> That's not what we rehearsed …

THE VOICE:
Since when are movies made by screenwriters? Directors make the movies. Not some broad sitting on her ass. Improvise, can't you? Your dialogue has gotta be as good as the dumb ass writer …

> **V.O.**
> But I thought —

THE VOICE:
Do we pay you to think? You're a professional, aren't you? Do you want the role or don't you — we're wasting overtime —

> **V.O.**
> Okay. The show … must go on. — Hey, guys, wait, these handcuffs are on awfully tight —

THE VOICE:
Come on! Let's finish this take ... Ready, lights, camera, action-

V.O.
(bad acting)
"Please don't hurt me ... "

THE VOICE:
I'm not gonna hurt you, baby ... I'm just gonna teach you a little lesson ... a lesson you'll remember ...
(There is the sound of a whip-lash)

V.O.
(Pain)
Shit! Wait a minute, guys — that really hurt. Larry — stop the camera — Larry? Where's Larry?

THE VOICE:
We told Larry to take a walk.

V.O.
(scared)
I don't know any of you guys ... are you guys with Gyno Productions?

THE VOICE:
This is not your screenplay.

V.O.
I don't understand.

THE VOICE:
Ever hear of snuff films?
(Just then, the bathroom door opens, and Charlene, in a peignoir, reenters the room. With a well-developed animal instinct, she stands stock-still, smelling the change in the air. Calvin and Leslie Ann have appeared as well, pressed against the window glass.

Calvin cries as he watches the live action, but Leslie Ann stands still and expressionless.)

THE VOICE:
What are you —

CLYDE:
What are you looking at?

CHARLENE:
(scared)
Nothing. Maybe this was a stupid idea.

THE VOICE:
You look ... great.

CLYDE:
You look ... great.

THE VOICE:
Really great.

CLYDE:
Really great.

CHARLENE:
Really? worth $18.37, huh?

THE VOICE:
Ya gotta have money to be a player.

CLYDE:
Let me ... hold you. Come here.

THE VOICE:
Lights, camera, action!
(Charlene goes to Clyde; they embrace.)

CHARLENE:
This feels good.

CLYDE:
You smell good.

V.O.
Get out of the house!

CLYDE:
I've been thinking — ya know, trying to figure out women. What turns them on. And I think tonight I've found the answer.

CHARLENE:
Let's not talk.
CLYDE:
Is it our smell? Our torso? Our butts?
CHARLENE:
Let's not bring that subject up.
(Charlene gently strokes Clyde's wounded behind and stops at the wetness.) Hey — wait a moment —
CLYDE:
I think women really get turned on to men in pain. That's what they like — (Charlene breaks away; in fear she examines her hand, now bloodied.)
CHARLENE:
Oh my god — Clyde, you're —
(Clyde reaches into the back of his pants, and rubs Charlene's face with his blood.) —
Oh my god —
(Charlene starts to dash for the hidden gun but Clyde is right on top of her. Clyde gets the gun away from Charlene.)
Clyde — listen —
CLYDE:
You. Goddamn. Whore!
(Clyde savagely hits Charlene.)
THE VOICE:
"She loved me for the dangers — " [14]
(As soon as Clyde strikes Charlene, in the next section, Clyde and Charlene lip-syncs the voices which are provided by The Voice and Voice-Over. The lip-syncs should be very crude; we watch their mouths move like puppets, mechanically and exaggerated.)

CLYDE:	**THE VOICE:**
(lip-sync)	(Live)
"Do you remember the last time?"	Do you remember the last time?
(Charlene starts to cry in elaborate pantomime.)	(The Voice-Over sobs into the microphone.)
CLYDE:	**THE VOICE:**
(lip-sync)	(Live)
"I asked you a question. Do. You. Remember. the last time."	I asked you a question. Do. You. Remember. the last time.

CHARLENE:
(lip-sync)
"When … we … made love?"
CLYDE:
(lip-sync)
"No. when I beat you to within
an inch of your life. You didn't
learn did you?"
CHARLENE:
(lip-sync)
"No."
CLYDE:
(lip-sync)
"I.can't.hear.you."
CHARLENE:
(lip-sync)
"No!"
CLYDE:
(Lip-sync)
"I'm going to have to
teach you all over again.
CHARLENE
(has difficulty breathing
and only shakes her head)
CLYDE:
(lip-syncs with difficulty)
"Get.On.The.bed."
CHARLENE:
(live, simultaneous)
Please —
CLYDE:
(lip-syncs)
"On.the.bed!"

V.O.
(Live)
When … we … made love?
THE VOICE:
(Live)
No. when I beat you to within
an inch of your life. You didn't
learn did you?
V.O.
(Live)
No.
THE VOICE:
(Live)
I.can't.hear.you.
V.O.
(Live)
No!
THE VOICE:
(Live)
I'm going to have to
teach you all over again.
V.O.
(Live)
Please — stop —
THE VOICE:
(Live)
Get.On.The.bed.
V.O.
(live, simultaneous)
Please —
THE VOICE:
(live)
On.the.bed!

(Clyde backhands Charlene and she falls on the bed.)
THE VOICE:
(whisper)
Now.don't.move.

CHARLENE:	V.O.
(live)	(live)
Don't.	Don't.
CLYDE:	**THE VOICE:**
(live)	(live)
Don't Move.	Don't Move.

(Clyde erupts into crying:)

CLYDE:

You're the one making me do this, Charlene. You shouldof never — never gotten that retraining order — kicked me out of my own house! Jesus Christ, Charlene — why did you do that? Why?

(Charlene reaches up to touch Clyde's face)

CHARLENE:

Don't cry — don't —

(Charlene tries to embrace Clyde)

(As Clyde unbuckles his belt, draws it from the loop, and wraps it around Charlene's throat, THE VOICE steps forward, reading from his own notes:)

THE VOICE:

"911 received a call at 9:30 am from victim's daughter. Arrived at the house approximately at 9:52. Victim: Charlene Dwyer, age 38. Pending coroner's report, strangulation appears to be cause of death. Time of death: 10-12 hours previous. Signs of forced entry. Alleged Perpetrator, Clyde Dwyer, age 42, found dead in bathroom of self-inflicted gunshot wound to the head. Pending forensic report, preliminary judgement: murder/suicide."

(Charlene recognizes the Detective. Charlene, for a moment, manages to wrest away from the belt's grip: she turns to Clyde.)

CHARLENE:

Why?!!

(Clyde redoubles his grip)

THE VOICE:

(whispered)

"Put out the Light and then Put out the light." [15]

(Clyde kills Charlene. For a moment, he cradles the body. The stage is empty save for the two of them. Clyde rocks Charlene's body, then lays the body down on the bed. He picks up the gun, checks it again, and exits to the bathroom. We hear a tape recording of the Voice reading:) "I asked him with my eyes to ask again yes and then he asked me would I yes to say yes my mountain flower and first I put my arms around his yes — "

(the tape recording slows down, warped, breaking down)

" ... and drew him down to me so he could feel my breasts all perfume yes and his heart was going like mad and yes I said yes I will Yes." [16]

(There is a flash of light. We hear a gunshot, Which reverberates as lights dim on the body of Charlene strewn across the bed.)

(A beat.)

Then, as the lights dim on Charlene's body, there is a bright spotlight outside the house, outside the playworld, into which Leslie Ann steps. She is dressed in a slip. Slowly, sensuously, she moves to music — something from the eighties that transposes into music from the nineties. But she is not dancing. She is dressing, slipping on a conservative dress. She steps into sensible heels. She smooths her stockings. She sweeps her hair up and back into a bun. If this play were a film script, we would see Leslie Ann age before our eyes. Her body becomes more worn, more protected from our gaze, her bones become less light, her face more determined.

Oh yes. She wears glasses. Just as she is about to speak to us, the recorded voice of Charlene cuts in:

CHARLENE'S VOICE-OVER

VOICE-OVER CONTINUED: FLASH-FOR-WARD. Twenty Years later. Leslie Ann finishes a lecture.

LESLIE ANN:

— At the end of today's class I will be collecting your papers on *Othello*. Next week we will continue our seminar on the Literature of Obsession with our reading of *Moby Dick* —

CHARLENE'S VOICE-OVER:

Moby Dick! I loved that book!

(Leslie Ann has paused, hearing her mother's voice. She continues a bit faster —)

LESLIE ANN:

My brother the screenwriter claims that *Moby Dick* is the one book that can not be adapted successfully by Hollywood. Be that as it may, many Ahabs in LA have tried ...

74

In the next four weeks, we will discuss not only Melville's master-piece, but the criticism of *Moby Dick,* which is as obsessive as the novel itself. We will examine how the book was first positioned as American in contrast to English literature by its juxtaposition of high and low culture, and its wild and erratic mixture of genres. During the Melville Revival, critics saw his similarity to modern writers, such as Joyce and D.H. Lawrence, in Melville's use of ambiguity, doubleness, the unreliability of the narrator, and stream of consciousness. We will discuss the myth critics, who saw *Moby Dick* as a Freudian tragedy that came from the repression of eros —

CHARLENE'S VOICE-OVER:
— You're going out of the house dressed like that and you blame me —

(Leslie Ann tries to concentrate)

LESLIE ANN:
— And we will sample the formalist, culturally materialist, deconstructivist and post-humanist —

CHARLENE'S VOICE-OVER
— Right. This. Minute. You are not leaving this house —

(Leslie Ann can't shut it out. For a moment it appears as if Leslie Ann will lose control in front of her class. She closes her eyes, and tries to gain composure)

LESLIE ANN:
— Excuse me. I can get very emotional when I talk about *Moby Dick.*
(Beat. She takes a breath, and then moves to dismiss her class:)
Okay. Your papers on *Moby Dick* will be due four weeks from today. As always, I expect you to be in control of your arguments, in control of your words, and in control —

(But Charlene again breaks into her daughter's stream of con-sciousness:)

CHARLENE'S VOICE-OVER:
(whispered)
Of your thoughts.

(Leslie Ann Dwyer freezes at the sound of her mother's voice.)

END OF PLAY

PROPERTY LIST

Books (in bookcase, including *Moby Dick*)
Catcher's mitt (VOICE-OVER)
Cigarette (VOICE-OVER)
Pack of cigarettes and matches (CHARLENE)
Hand gun (CHARLENE)
Bandages (CHARLENE)
Tape (CHARLENE)
Antiseptic bottle (CHARLENE)
2 coffee cups (CHARLENE)
Business card (CHARLENE)
Remy bottle and 2 shot glasses (CHARLENE)
Tray (CHARLENE)
Coffee pot (CHARLENE)
2 mugs (CHARLENE)
Plate of cookies (CHARLENE)
Glass of milk (CHARLENE)
Sleeping bag (LESLIE ANN)
Film slate (VOICE)
Five-dollar bill (CLYDE)
Condom (VOICE)

SOUND EFFECTS

Water running
Automobile horn
Door keys and slam
Whip-lash
Voice on tape
Gunshots

CITATIONS

1. Eric Clapton and Jim Gordon, "Layla," recorded by Derek and the Dominos, 1970.
2. Vladimir Nabokov, *Lolita*, Vintage International Books, New York, 1989.
3. Herman Melville, *Moby-Dick or The Whale*, Penguin Books, New York, 1992.
4. ibid.
5. D.H. Lawrence, *Lady Chatterly's Lover*, Grove Press, New York, 1959.
6. Henry Miller, *Plexus*, Grove Press, New York, 1965.
7. William Shakespeare, *Othello*, Yale University Press, New Haven, 1965.
8. *Plexus.*
9. James Joyce, *Ulysses,* Garland Publishing, Inc., New York, 1984.
10. ibid.
11. ibid.
12. *Plexus.*
13. Jay Anson and Sandor Stern, *The Amityville Horror*, 1979.
14. *Othello.*
15. ibid.
16. *Ulysses.*

NEW PLAYS

★ **MATCH by Stephen Belber.** Mike and Lisa Davis interview a dancer and choreographer about his life, but it is soon evident that their agenda will either ruin or inspire them— and definitely change their lives forever. "Prolific laughs and ear-to-ear smiles." *–NY Magazine.* "Uproariously funny, deeply moving, enthralling theater. Stephen Belber's MATCH has great beauty and tenderness, and abounds in wit." *–NY Daily News.* "Three and a half out of four stars." *–USA Today.* "A theatrical steeplechase that leads straight from outrageous bitchery to unadorned, heartfelt emotion." *–Wall Street Journal.* [2M, 1W] ISBN: 0-8222-2020-2

★ **HANK WILLIAMS: LOST HIGHWAY by Randal Myler and Mark Harelik.** The story of the beloved and volatile country-music legend Hank Williams, featuring twenty-five of his most unforgettable songs. "[LOST HIGHWAY has] the exhilarating feeling of Williams on stage in a particular place on a particular night…serves up classic country with the edges raw and the energy hot…By the end of the play, you've traveled on a profound emotional journey: LOST HIGHWAY transports its audience and communicates the inspiring message of the beauty and richness of Williams' songs…forceful, clear-eyed, moving, impressive." *–Rolling Stone.* "…honors a very particular musical talent with care and energy… smart, sweet, poignant." *–NY Times.* [7M, 3W] ISBN: 0-8222-1985-9

★ **THE STORY by Tracey Scott Wilson.** An ambitious black newspaper reporter goes against her editor to investigate a murder and finds the *best* story…but at what cost? "A singular new voice…deeply emotional, deeply intellectual, and deeply musical…" *–The New Yorker.* "…a conscientious and absorbing new drama…" *–NY Times.* "…a riveting, tough-minded drama about race, reporting and the truth…" *–A.P.* "… a stylish, attention-holding script that ends on a chilling note that will leave viewers with much to talk about." *–Curtain Up.* [2M, 7W (doubling, flexible casting)] ISBN: 0-8222-1998-0

★ **OUR LADY OF 121st STREET by Stephen Adly Guirgis.** The body of Sister Rose, beloved Harlem nun, has been stolen, reuniting a group of life-challenged childhood friends who square off as they wait for her return. "A scorching and dark new comedy…" Mr. Guirgis has one of the finest imaginations for dialogue to come along in years." *–NY Times.* "Stephen Guirgis may be the best playwright in America under forty." *–NY Magazine.* [8M, 4W] ISBN: 0-8222-1965-4

★ **HOLLYWOOD ARMS by Carrie Hamilton and Carol Burnett.** The coming-of-age story of a dreamer who manages to escape her bleak life and follow her romantic ambitions to stardom. Based on Carol Burnett's bestselling autobiography, *One More Time.* "…pure theatre and pure entertainment…" *–Talkin' Broadway.* "…a warm, fuzzy evening of theatre." *–BrodwayBeat.com.* "…chuckles and smiles of recognition or surprise flow naturally…a remarkable slice of life." *–TheatreScene.net.* [5M, 5W, 1 girl] ISBN: 0-8222-1959-X

★ **INVENTING VAN GOGH by Steven Dietz.** A haunting and hallucinatory drama about the making of art, the obsession to create and the fine line that separates truth from myth. "Like a van Gogh painting, Dietz's story is a gorgeous example of excess—one that remakes reality with broad, well-chosen brush strokes. At evening's end, we're left with the author's resounding opinions on art and artifice, and provoked by his constant query into which is greater: van Gogh's art or his violent myth." *–Phoenix New Times.* "Dietz's writing is never simple. It is always brilliant. Shaded, compressed, direct, lucid—he frames his subject with a remarkable understanding of painting as a physical experience." *–Tucson Citizen.* [4M, 1W] ISBN: 0-8222-1954-9

DRAMATISTS PLAY SERVICE, INC.
440 Park Avenue South, New York, NY 10016   212-683-8960 Fax 212-213-1539
postmaster@dramatists.com   www.dramatists.com

NEW PLAYS

★ **INTIMATE APPAREL by Lynn Nottage.** The moving and lyrical story of a turn-of-the-century black seamstress whose gifted hands and sewing machine are the tools she uses to fashion her dreams from the whole cloth of her life's experiences. "…Nottage's play has a delicacy and eloquence that seem absolutely right for the time she is depicting…" *–NY Daily News.* "…thoughtful, affecting…The play offers poignant commentary on an era when the cut and color of one's dress—and of course, skin—determined whom one could and could not marry, sleep with, even talk to in public." *–Variety.* [2M, 4W] ISBN: 0-8222-2009-1

★ **BROOKLYN BOY by Donald Margulies.** A witty and insightful look at what happens to a writer when his novel hits the bestseller list. "The characters are beautifully drawn, the dialogue sparkles…" *–nytheatre.com.* "Few playwrights have the mastery to smartly investigate so much through a laugh-out-loud comedy that combines the vintage subject matter of successful writer-returning-to-ethnic-roots with the familiar mid-life crisis." *–Show Business Weekly.* [4M, 3W] ISBN: 0-8222-2074-1

★ **CROWNS by Regina Taylor.** Hats become a springboard for an exploration of black history and identity in this celebratory musical play. "Taylor pulls off a Hat Trick: She scores thrice, turning CROWNS into an artful amalgamation of oral history, fashion show, and musical theater…" *–TheatreMania.com.* "…wholly theatrical…Ms. Taylor has created a show that seems to arise out of spontaneous combustion, as if a bevy of department-store customers simultaneously decided to stage a revival meeting in the changing room." *–NY Times.* [1M, 6W (2 musicians)] ISBN: 0-8222-1963-8

★ **EXITS AND ENTRANCES by Athol Fugard.** The story of a relationship between a young playwright on the threshold of his career and an aging actor who has reached the end of his. "[Fugard] can say more with a single line than most playwrights convey in an entire script…Paraphrasing the title, it's safe to say this drama, making its memorable entrance into our consciousness, is unlikely to exit as long as a theater exists for exceptional work." *–Variety.* "A thought-provoking, elegant and engrossing new play…" *–Hollywood Reporter.* [2M] ISBN: 0-8222-2041-5

★ **BUG by Tracy Letts.** A thriller featuring a pair of star-crossed lovers in an Oklahoma City motel facing a bug invasion, paranoia, conspiracy theories and twisted psychological motives. "…obscenely exciting…top-flight craftsmanship. Buckle up and brace yourself…" *–NY Times.* "…[a] thoroughly outrageous and thoroughly entertaining play…the possibility of enemies, real and imagined, to squash has never been more theatrical." *–A.P.* [3M, 2W] ISBN: 0-8222-2016-4

★ **THOM PAIN (BASED ON NOTHING) by Will Eno.** An ordinary man muses on childhood, yearning, disappointment and loss, as he draws the audience into his last-ditch plea for empathy and enlightenment. "It's one of those treasured nights in the theater—treasured nights anywhere, for that matter—that can leave you both breathless with exhilaration and…in a puddle of tears." *–NY Times.* "Eno's words…are familiar, but proffered in a way that is constantly contradictory to our expectations. Beckett is certainly among his literary ancestors." *–nytheatre.com.* [1M] ISBN: 0-8222-2076-8

★ **THE LONG CHRISTMAS RIDE HOME by Paula Vogel.** Past, present and future collide on a snowy Christmas Eve for a troubled family of five. "…[a] lovely and hauntingly original family drama…a work that breathes so much life into the theater." *–Time Out.* "…[a] delicate visual feast…" *–NY Times.* "…brutal and lovely…the overall effect is magical." *–NY Newsday.* [3M, 3W] ISBN: 0-8222-2003-2

DRAMATISTS PLAY SERVICE, INC.
440 Park Avenue South, New York, NY 10016 212-683-8960 Fax 212-213-1539
postmaster@dramatists.com www.dramatists.com